DAN CAMPBELL'S COACHING STRATEGIES

Success On And Off The Gridiron

Myers Shah

All rights reserved. No part of this publication may be reproduced, distributed, or transmitted in any form or by any means, including photocopying, recording, or other electronic or mechanical methods, without the prior written permission of the publisher, except in the case of brief quotations embodied in critical reviews and certain other noncommercial uses permitted by copyright law.

Copyright © Myers Shah 2024

TABLE OF CONTENTS

INTRODUCTION

CHAPTER ONE: Early Life and Education

CHAPTER TWO: Playing Career

CHAPTER THREE: Coaching Career

CHAPTER FOUR: Personal Life and Family

CHAPTER FIVE: Philanthropy and Community Involvement

CHAPTER SIX: Legacy and Impact

Influence on Players and Coaching Staff

Media and Public Perception

INTRODUCTION

Dan Campbell, a name synonymous with grit, passion, and resilience, has carved out a unique and respected niche in the world of American football. Born on April 13, 1976, in Clifton, Texas, Campbell's journey from a small-town athlete to a formidable NFL player and dynamic head coach is a story of unwavering determination and relentless pursuit of excellence. Known for his intense coaching style and unyielding commitment to his teams, Campbell has become a beloved figure both on and off the field.

Campbell's early life was steeped in the values of hard work and perseverance, traits that would later define his professional career. Growing up in a tight-knit community, he developed a deep love for football, a sport that would become his lifelong passion. His high school success paved the way for a standout collegiate career at Texas A&M, where his leadership and athleticism quickly caught the attention of NFL scouts.

Drafted by the New York Giants in the third round of the 1999 NFL Draft, Campbell embarked on a decade-long playing career that saw him don the jerseys of several teams, including the Dallas Cowboys, Detroit Lions, and New Orleans Saints. As a tight end, he was known for his rugged playing style, dependable blocking, and clutch performances in crucial moments. His time as a player was marked by a deep understanding of the game, which seamlessly transitioned into his coaching career.

After hanging up his cleats, Campbell's passion for football led him to the sidelines, where he began to impart his knowledge and experience to a new generation of players. His coaching journey started with the Miami Dolphins, where he quickly made a name for himself as an inspiring leader and innovative strategist. His tenure as the interim head coach in 2015 showcased his ability to galvanize a team and compete at the highest level.

In 2021, Campbell took on the role of head coach for the Detroit Lions, bringing his trademark intensity and vision to a franchise in need of revitalization. His coaching philosophy, built on principles of toughness, accountability, and teamwork, has begun to reshape the culture of the Lions, earning him the admiration and respect of players, fans, and analysts alike.

Beyond the Xs and Os, Dan Campbell's impact extends to his personal life, where he is known for his philanthropic efforts and deep commitment to community service. His authenticity and genuine care for those around him have endeared him to many, making him not just a coach, but a mentor and role model.

Dan Campbell's story is not just one of personal achievement, but also a testament to the transformative power of leadership and the impact one individual can have on an entire organization. From his early days as a player known for his relentless work ethic and dedication, to his current role as a head coach tasked with turning around a storied but struggling franchise, Campbell's journey offers valuable insights into the nature of success and the qualities that define great leaders.

His tenure with the Miami Dolphins marked a significant chapter in his coaching career. As an assistant coach, he was instrumental in developing players and fostering a competitive environment. When he was named interim head coach in 2015, his fiery passion and no-nonsense approach quickly garnered respect from players and fans. Under his leadership, the Dolphins showed a marked improvement in their performance and attitude, a testament to Campbell's ability to inspire and motivate.

The transition to the Detroit Lions represented both a new challenge and a new opportunity for Campbell. Taking the helm of a team with a rich history but recent struggles, he faced the daunting task of rebuilding not just the roster, but also the culture of the organization. His introductory press conference set the tone for his tenure, with his now-famous declaration that his team would "bite a kneecap off" if knocked down, encapsulating his tough, relentless mindset.

Under Campbell's guidance, the Lions have begun to show signs of a turnaround. His focus on building a resilient, hard-working team that embodies the spirit of Detroit has resonated with the city's blue-collar ethos. His ability to connect with players on a personal level, understanding their motivations and challenges, has fostered a sense of unity and purpose within the team. As a coach, he emphasizes the importance of playing with heart and determination, qualities that he himself exemplified throughout his playing career.

Off the field, Campbell's commitment to his community and charitable work further highlights his character. Whether it's supporting local initiatives or engaging in philanthropic efforts, he consistently strives to make a positive impact beyond the gridiron. This dedication to giving back underscores the values that have guided him throughout his life and career.

From his early influences and playing days to his rise through the coaching ranks and current role with the Lions, Campbell's story is one of perseverance, passion, and an unwavering commitment to excellence. His legacy, still being written, offers valuable lessons for anyone aspiring to lead, inspire, and make a lasting difference.

CHAPTER ONE: Early Life and Education

Dan Campbell's journey to the NFL and coaching prominence began in the modest town of Clifton, Texas, where he was born on April 13, 1976. Growing up in this rural community, Campbell was immersed in a culture that valued hard work, resilience, and community—a backdrop that would significantly shape his character and approach to life.

Childhood and Family Background

Raised in a close-knit family, Campbell was instilled with a strong sense of values from an early age. His parents emphasized the importance of dedication, integrity, and perseverance, traits that Campbell would carry with him throughout his career. His father, Larry Campbell, was a welder, and his mother, Betty Campbell, was a homemaker. Their work ethic and support played a crucial role in molding Dan into a determined and hardworking individual.

As a child, Campbell was naturally drawn to sports, with football quickly becoming his passion. In a town where Friday night lights were a cherished tradition, Campbell thrived in the local sports scene. His early experiences on the football field were characterized by a raw intensity and love for the game, foreshadowing the fervor he would later bring to his professional career.

Education and Early Interests

Campbell attended Glen Rose High School, where he was a standout athlete. Playing for the Glen Rose Tigers, he excelled in both football and track and field. As a tight end and defensive end, Campbell's physicality and leadership were evident, earning him recognition and accolades. His high school career was marked by numerous achievements, including All-State honors, which put him on the radar of college scouts.

In addition to his athletic prowess, Campbell was a dedicated student. He understood the importance of education and balanced his academic responsibilities with his athletic commitments. This discipline and focus would serve him well in the competitive world of college football and beyond.

College Football at Texas A&M

After graduating from high school, Campbell received a scholarship to play football at Texas A&M University, a testament to his talent and potential. At Texas A&M, he joined the Aggies football program, where he continued to develop his skills and solidify his reputation as a formidable player. Under the guidance of head coach R.C. Slocum, Campbell's college career flourished.

Playing as a tight end for the Aggies from 1995 to 1998, Campbell was known for his versatility, strong blocking, and reliable hands. His performance on the field earned him respect from teammates and coaches alike. Off the field, Campbell pursued a degree in agricultural development, reflecting his appreciation for his rural roots and a desire to stay connected to his upbringing.

During his time at Texas A&M, Campbell's leadership qualities began to shine through. He was not only a key player but also a mentor and motivator for his teammates. His ability to inspire those around him and his commitment to the team were early indicators of the coaching career that lay ahead.

Influences and Mentors

Throughout his formative years, Campbell was influenced by several mentors who helped shape his approach to football and life. Coaches, teachers, and family members all played pivotal roles in guiding him and nurturing his development. At Texas A&M, head coach R.C.

Slocum's emphasis on discipline, teamwork, and perseverance left a lasting impression on Campbell, providing a blueprint for his future coaching philosophy.

Campbell's early life and education were marked by a combination of talent, hard work, and influential mentorship. These elements laid the foundation for his successful playing career and eventual transition into coaching. His journey from a small-town athlete to a respected figure in the NFL is a testament to the enduring impact of his upbringing and the values instilled in him from a young age. As we delve deeper into his career, the lessons and experiences from his early life continue to resonate, shaping the leader he has become.

Dan Campbell's tenure at Texas A&M University was pivotal in shaping his future both on and off the field. As a member of the Aggies, he played under the watchful eye of Coach R.C. Slocum, whose emphasis on discipline, toughness, and teamwork left an indelible mark on Campbell's coaching philosophy. Campbell's contributions to the team were multifaceted, and his performance on the field was nothing short of exemplary.

Playing Career at Texas A&M

During his college career from 1995 to 1998, Campbell stood out as a versatile and formidable tight end. His size, athleticism, and football IQ made him a standout player in the Big 12 Conference. Campbell's blocking skills were particularly noteworthy, allowing him to excel in both run and pass plays. His ability to create opportunities for his teammates, combined with his knack for making crucial catches, earned him the respect of both coaches and peers.

Campbell's senior year in 1998 was especially remarkable. He recorded impressive statistics, showcasing his versatility and reliability. His performance on the field was critical in helping the Aggies secure important victories, and his leadership qualities were evident in his role as a team captain. Campbell's contributions helped Texas A&M achieve a high national ranking, and his exploits on the field cemented his status as one of the top tight ends in college football.

Academic Pursuits and Development

Beyond his athletic achievements, Campbell was a dedicated student. He pursued a degree in agricultural development, a nod to his Texas roots and his desire to stay connected to the land and rural lifestyle that shaped him. His academic journey was characterized by a strong work ethic and a commitment to excellence, balancing his studies with his athletic commitments. This balance of academics and athletics helped hone his time-management skills and his ability to perform under pressure, qualities that would prove invaluable in his future coaching career.

Mentorship and Leadership

During his college years, Campbell was mentored by several influential figures who helped guide his development. Coach R.C. Slocum, in particular, played a crucial role in shaping Campbell's approach to the game and to life. Slocum's emphasis on character, integrity, and hard work resonated with Campbell, instilling in him the values that would define his coaching philosophy. Campbell also drew inspiration from his position coach, who taught him the nuances of the tight end position and the importance of being a well-rounded player.

Campbell's leadership skills were evident both on and off the field. He was known for his ability to inspire and motivate his teammates, often leading by example with his work ethic, determination, and positive attitude. His contributions to the team went beyond his on-field performance; he was a mentor to younger players, offering guidance and support that helped build a cohesive and motivated team.

Legacy at Texas A&M
Dan Campbell's legacy at Texas A&M is one of toughness, leadership, and excellence. His

impact on the program extended beyond his playing days, as his work ethic and commitment to the team's success left a lasting impression on everyone associated with the Aggies. His name remains synonymous with the spirit of Texas A&M football, and his contributions continue to be celebrated by fans, coaches, and former teammates.

As Campbell transitioned from college to the professional ranks, the foundation laid at Texas A&M proved to be crucial. The lessons learned, the values instilled, and the relationships forged during his time at the university played a significant role in shaping the coach he would become. His journey from a determined college athlete to an influential NFL coach is a testament to the enduring impact of his early experiences and the solid groundwork laid during his college years.

CHAPTER TWO: Playing Career

Dan Campbell's playing career in the NFL spanned a decade, marked by a reputation for toughness, reliability, and a deep understanding of the game. Drafted in the third round of the 1999 NFL Draft, Campbell's journey through the league saw him contribute significantly to several teams, earning respect as a formidable tight end known for his blocking and leadership skills.

New York Giants (1999-2002)

Campbell was selected by the New York Giants in the third round (79th overall pick) of the 1999 NFL Draft. Joining a team with a storied history and a passionate fan base, Campbell quickly made his presence felt. As a rookie, he played in 12 games, making an immediate impact with his blocking abilities and special teams contributions.

In the 2000 season, Campbell played a key role in the Giants' journey to Super Bowl XXXV. Although primarily known for his blocking, he contributed as a receiver when needed, showcasing his versatility. His role as a reliable tight end and his work ethic earned him the trust of his coaches and teammates. The Giants' Super Bowl run, although ending in a loss to the Baltimore Ravens, was a significant early highlight in Campbell's career.

Dallas Cowboys (2003-2005)

In 2003, Campbell signed with the Dallas Cowboys, a move that brought him to one of the NFL's most storied franchises. Under head coach Bill Parcells, Campbell found a mentor who valued his tough, no-nonsense approach to the game. Parcells' influence on Campbell was profound, as he was known for emphasizing discipline and physicality—qualities that Campbell embodied.

During his time with the Cowboys, Campbell continued to excel as a blocking tight end, often serving as an additional lineman in running plays. His contributions were crucial in protecting the quarterback and opening lanes for running backs. Campbell's leadership and veteran presence were invaluable to a team undergoing significant changes, and his consistency helped stabilize the offense.

Detroit Lions (2006-2008)

Campbell's next stop was with the Detroit Lions, where he played from 2006 to 2008. Despite the team's struggles during this period, Campbell's performance remained steadfast. He brought experience and leadership to a young Lions team, providing mentorship to younger players and contributing both on and off the field.

In his first season with the Lions, Campbell had a career year as a receiver, catching 21 passes for 308 yards and four touchdowns. His ability to contribute in the passing game, combined with his exceptional blocking, made him a valuable asset. Campbell's time in Detroit, although challenging in terms of team success, highlighted his resilience and dedication to the sport.

New Orleans Saints (2009)

In 2009, Campbell signed with the New Orleans Saints. However, his time with the team was short-lived due to injuries. Despite not playing a significant role on the field, Campbell's experience and knowledge were assets to the Saints' locker room. His understanding of the game and his ability to mentor younger players continued to be invaluable.

Playing Style and Impact

Dan Campbell's playing style was characterized by his physicality, toughness, and selflessness. As a tight end, he excelled in blocking, often acting as an extension of the offensive line. His ability to protect the quarterback and create running lanes was crucial to the success of the offenses he played for. While not known for prolific receiving numbers, Campbell's reliability in clutch situations and his ability to make key catches when needed were significant aspects of his game.

Off the field, Campbell was respected for his leadership and work ethic. His teammates viewed him as a consummate professional who led by example. His dedication to preparation, willingness to put the team's needs above his own, and ability to inspire those around him were hallmarks of his career.

Transition to Coaching

Campbell's transition from player to coach was a natural progression, given his deep understanding of the game and his leadership qualities. The lessons he learned as a player—discipline, resilience, and the importance of teamwork—became foundational elements of his coaching philosophy. His experience playing under influential coaches like Bill Parcells and R.C. Slocum provided him with a wealth of knowledge and a diverse perspective on leadership and strategy.

As Campbell moved into coaching, he carried with him the same passion and intensity that defined his playing career. His journey as a player laid a strong foundation for his subsequent success as a coach, and his experiences on the field continue to inform his approach to leading and inspiring the next generation of football players.

Dan Campbell's playing career is a testament to the values of hard work, perseverance, and leadership. From his early days with the New

York Giants to his role as a veteran leader with the Detroit Lions, Campbell's contributions to the NFL were significant and enduring. His journey from player to coach is a reflection of his deep love for the game and his unwavering commitment to excellence.

Transition to Coaching

Dan Campbell's transition from an NFL player to a coach was a natural progression, given his extensive experience and deep understanding of the game. His playing career not only prepared him for coaching but also instilled in him a unique perspective on leadership, strategy, and team dynamics.

Early Coaching Experience

After retiring as a player, Campbell quickly pivoted to coaching, beginning his new career with the Miami Dolphins. In 2010, he was hired as the team's assistant coach, focusing on the tight ends. Under the guidance of head coach Tony Sparano, Campbell's transition was marked by his enthusiasm and dedication. His ability to mentor younger players and his attention to detail were immediately evident, helping him build a strong reputation as an up-and-coming coach.

During his time with the Dolphins, Campbell's impact was felt both on and off the field. His hands-on approach and willingness to work closely with his players made him a valuable asset to the coaching staff. His emphasis on fundamentals, coupled with his ability to relate to players through his own experiences, helped improve the performance and development of the tight ends he coached.

Miami Dolphins: Interim Head Coach

In December 2015, following the dismissal of head coach Joe Philbin, Campbell was named interim head coach of the Miami Dolphins. This role marked a significant milestone in Campbell's coaching career. Despite stepping into the role under challenging circumstances, Campbell's leadership qualities and his ability to inspire the team were on full display.

Campbell's tenure as interim head coach was characterized by a renewed sense of energy and motivation within the team. His famous press conference, where he vowed that the team would "bite a kneecap off" if knocked down, became a defining moment and exemplified his aggressive, no-holds-barred approach to coaching. Under his leadership, the Dolphins showed improved performance and resilience, ending the season with a 5-7 record under his guidance. Although the Dolphins did not make the playoffs, Campbell's tenure was seen as a positive step in demonstrating his potential as a head coach.

New Orleans Saints: Assistant Head Coach and Tight Ends Coach

In 2016, Campbell joined the New Orleans Saints as the assistant head coach and tight ends coach, a role that allowed him to continue developing his coaching skills under the mentorship of head coach Sean Payton. At the Saints, Campbell was part of a successful coaching staff that helped the team achieve several playoff berths.

His role involved working closely with the tight ends, focusing on their development and performance. Campbell's ability to connect with his players and his understanding of the tight end position were instrumental in the success of the Saints' offense. His contributions were crucial in maintaining the high standards of the team and further solidified his reputation as a knowledgeable and effective coach.

Detroit Lions: Head Coach

In January 2021, Dan Campbell was hired as the head coach of the Detroit Lions, marking a new chapter in his career. The Lions, a franchise with a storied history but recent struggles, presented Campbell with a significant challenge. His appointment was met with optimism and curiosity from fans and analysts alike.

Campbell's first season as head coach was a period of rebuilding and reestablishing the team's culture. He brought his signature intensity and enthusiasm to the role, emphasizing a tough, physical style of play and fostering a culture of accountability and resilience. His approach was reflected in the team's performance and the improvement in their competitive spirit.

One of Campbell's notable achievements during his early tenure was his ability to connect with his players on a personal level. His leadership style, characterized by honesty, passion, and a commitment to player development, quickly won him the respect of the team. Despite the challenges faced during his initial seasons, Campbell's efforts to instill a winning mentality and his strategic acumen were evident.

Dan Campbell's coaching career has been marked by a combination of passion, resilience, and a deep understanding of the game. His experiences as a player have profoundly influenced his coaching philosophy, shaping his approach to leadership and team-building. His ability to inspire, mentor, and develop players has been a key factor in his success as a coach.

As Campbell continues to lead the Detroit Lions, his impact on the team and the broader football community is evident. His dedication to building a strong, competitive team and his commitment to fostering a positive and motivated locker room are hallmarks of his coaching career. Campbell's journey from player to head coach is a testament to his enduring love for the game and his unwavering dedication to excellence.

Dan Campbell's coaching career has been a remarkable continuation of his football journey. From his early days with the Miami Dolphins to his role with the New Orleans Saints and his current position with the Detroit Lions, Campbell's contributions to the sport reflect his deep passion for football and his commitment to making a lasting impact. His evolution from a respected player to a successful coach exemplifies the values of hard work, leadership, and dedication that have defined his career.

CHAPTER THREE: Coaching Career

Dan Campbell's coaching career is a testament to his deep understanding of football, his commitment to player development, and his ability to lead and inspire teams. From his early days as an assistant coach to his current role as head coach of the Detroit Lions, Campbell's journey through the coaching ranks reflects his passion for the game and his unwavering dedication to excellence.

Early Coaching Experience with the Miami Dolphins

Dan Campbell began his coaching career in 2010 with the Miami Dolphins, where he initially served as the tight ends coach. This role marked the beginning of Campbell's transition from player to coach, allowing him to leverage his playing experience to mentor and develop younger players.

Under head coach Tony Sparano, Campbell's coaching style was characterized by his enthusiasm, attention to detail, and a hands-on approach. His work with the Dolphins' tight ends was marked by his ability to impart fundamental skills, improve blocking techniques, and foster a competitive atmosphere. Campbell's deep knowledge of the game, gained from his years as a player, enabled him to connect with his players on a personal level and enhance their performance.

In 2015, Campbell was elevated to the role of interim head coach after Sparano's dismissal. This promotion was a significant milestone in Campbell's coaching career. Despite the challenging circumstances, Campbell's leadership qualities came to the forefront. His famous press conference, where he declared that the team would "bite a kneecap off" if knocked down, became a defining moment of his tenure. Under his guidance, the Dolphins showed improved performance and competitiveness, reflecting Campbell's ability to motivate and inspire his team.

New Orleans Saints: Assistant Head Coach and Tight Ends Coach

In 2016, Campbell joined the New Orleans Saints as the assistant head coach and tight ends coach. This role provided him with an opportunity to work under the esteemed head coach Sean Payton, further honing his coaching skills and expanding his understanding of team management and strategy.

Campbell's tenure with the Saints was marked by his focus on player development and his contributions to the team's offensive success. His work with the tight ends continued to be a highlight, as he helped shape a key component of the Saints' high-powered offense. Campbell's ability to build strong relationships with his players, coupled with his deep football acumen, made him an invaluable member of the coaching staff.

The Saints' success during Campbell's time with the team, including multiple playoff appearances, was a testament to his contributions. His role as assistant head coach allowed him to gain experience in broader aspects of team management, including game planning and strategic decision-making. This experience was instrumental in preparing him for future head coaching opportunities.

Detroit Lions: Head Coach

In January 2021, Dan Campbell was hired as the head coach of the Detroit Lions, marking a new chapter in his coaching career. The Lions, a franchise with a rich history but recent struggles, presented Campbell with a significant challenge. His appointment was met with optimism and anticipation from fans and analysts eager to see how his leadership style and coaching philosophy would impact the team.

Campbell's first season with the Lions was characterized by his intense and passionate approach to coaching. He emphasized a tough, physical style of play, instilling a sense of resilience and determination within the team. His leadership style was marked by honesty, transparency, and a commitment to building strong relationships with his players. Campbell's ability to connect with his team on a personal level, combined with his strategic insights, quickly earned him the respect of the Lions' locker room.

One of Campbell's key achievements in his early tenure with the Lions was his ability to foster a positive and motivated team culture. Despite the team's challenges, including a rebuilding phase and a tough schedule, Campbell's focus on player development and team unity helped improve the team's performance and competitiveness. His emphasis on playing with heart and grit resonated with both players and fans, reflecting his deep commitment to the Lions' long-term success.

Campbell's coaching philosophy is characterized by a blend of intensity, accountability, and adaptability. He values hard work, discipline, and a team-first mentality, and he continuously seeks to inspire his players to give their best effort. His approach to coaching reflects his own experiences as a player, including the lessons he learned from influential mentors and coaches throughout his career.

Dan Campbell's coaching career has been marked by his dedication to building strong, competitive teams and his commitment to developing players both on and off the field. His journey from assistant coach to head coach reflects his deep passion for football and his unwavering determination to make a positive impact.

As Campbell continues to lead the Detroit Lions, his influence on the team and the broader football community is evident. His ability to inspire, motivate, and connect with players is a testament to his leadership and coaching skills. Campbell's career is a reflection of his love for the game, his commitment to excellence, and his dedication to making a lasting difference in the sport.

Dan Campbell's coaching career is a story of growth, dedication, and impact. From his early days with the Miami Dolphins to his role with the New Orleans Saints and his current position with the Detroit Lions, Campbell's contributions to football have been significant and enduring. His journey as a coach is a testament to his passion for the game and his commitment to leading and inspiring the next generation of football players.

Key Moments and Challenges

Dan Campbell's coaching career has been punctuated by significant moments and challenges that have shaped his approach and reputation. Each phase of his career has contributed to his development as a head coach and provided valuable lessons that continue to influence his leadership style.

Resilience and Adaptability: One of the defining aspects of Campbell's coaching career has been his resilience and adaptability in the face of challenges. Whether dealing with the turnover and instability in Miami or navigating the rebuilding phase in Detroit, Campbell has demonstrated an ability to remain focused and positive. His approach to adversity reflects his belief in the importance of maintaining a strong mindset and staying committed to long-term goals.

Building a Winning Culture: At the Detroit Lions, Campbell's primary focus has been on building a winning culture and establishing a new identity for the team. His emphasis on physicality, discipline, and accountability has been central to this effort. Campbell's approach involves instilling a sense of pride and commitment in his players, encouraging them to embrace a competitive mindset and strive for excellence.

Player Development: Throughout his coaching career, Campbell has been dedicated to player development. His ability to mentor and nurture young talent has been a hallmark of his career. In Detroit, Campbell has worked closely with players to help them reach their full potential, providing guidance, support, and constructive feedback. His hands-on approach and personalized coaching have contributed to the growth and improvement of individual players and the team as a whole.

Coaching Philosophy and Style

Dan Campbell's coaching philosophy is deeply rooted in his experiences as a player and his understanding of the game. His philosophy emphasizes several core principles:

1. Physicality and Toughness: Campbell places a strong emphasis on physical play and toughness. He believes that a successful team must be resilient, both physically and mentally, and must be willing to outwork opponents. This emphasis on physicality is reflected in his team's style of play and practice routines.

2. Accountability and Discipline: Accountability is a key component of Campbell's coaching philosophy. He holds players to high standards of performance and behavior, expecting them to take responsibility for their actions and their contributions to the team. Discipline is a cornerstone of his approach, with a focus on ensuring that players adhere to team rules and guidelines.

3. Building Relationships: Campbell's leadership style is characterized by his ability to build strong relationships with his players. He values open communication and strives to connect with each player on a personal level. By understanding their motivations and challenges, Campbell is able to provide effective support and guidance.

4. Adaptability and Innovation: Campbell's experience with various teams and coaching staff has taught him the importance of adaptability and innovation. He is open to new ideas and approaches, constantly seeking ways to improve and evolve. This adaptability allows him to tailor his strategies to the strengths and weaknesses of his team and opponents.

Community Engagement and Leadership

Beyond his coaching responsibilities, Dan Campbell has been actively involved in community engagement and leadership. His commitment to giving back to the community is an important aspect of his career and personal values. Campbell has participated in various charitable initiatives and community outreach programs, using his platform to make a positive impact.

His involvement in community service reflects his belief in the importance of contributing to society and supporting those in need. Campbell's leadership extends beyond the football field, demonstrating his dedication to making a difference in the lives of others and fostering a sense of responsibility and service within his team.

As Dan Campbell continues to lead the Detroit Lions, the future of his coaching career holds great potential. His dedication to building a competitive team and his commitment to player development are likely to drive continued progress and success. Campbell's approach to coaching, characterized by his passion, resilience, and focus on building a strong team culture, positions him well for future achievements.

The journey of Dan Campbell's coaching career is one of growth, learning, and impact. From his early days as an assistant coach to his role as head coach of the Detroit Lions, Campbell's contributions to football have been significant and enduring. His coaching philosophy, leadership style, and commitment to player development have shaped his career and continue to influence the sport.

Dan Campbell's coaching career is a testament to his dedication, passion, and expertise. His journey through various coaching roles, his emphasis on physicality and discipline, and his commitment to building strong relationships with players reflect his deep understanding of the game and his desire to make a positive impact. As Campbell looks to the future, his legacy as a coach will be defined by his continued efforts to inspire, lead, and build successful teams.

CHAPTER FOUR:
Personal Life and Family

Dan Campbell's personal life and family background provide a rich context for understanding the man behind the coach. His experiences growing up, his relationships with family, and his personal interests have significantly influenced his approach to life and football.

Dan Campbell was born on April 13, 1976, in Clifton, Texas. His upbringing in this small town was shaped by a strong sense of community and the values of hard work and perseverance. Raised in a close-knit family, Campbell was instilled with a sense of discipline and responsibility from an early age.

Parents and Siblings: Campbell's father, Larry Campbell, worked as a welder, while his mother, Betty Campbell, was a homemaker. The values they imparted—emphasizing the importance of integrity, effort, and dedication—played a crucial role in shaping Dan's character. His parents' work ethic and supportive nature provided a stable foundation for his growth and development.

Dan Campbell also has a brother, who has been a source of personal support and shared experiences. Growing up in a family that valued hard work and mutual support, Campbell learned early on the importance of loyalty and teamwork—lessons that would later become integral to his coaching philosophy.

Marriage and Children

Dan Campbell is married to his high school sweetheart, Holly Campbell. The couple has been together for many years, and their relationship has been a cornerstone of Campbell's personal life. Holly has been a supportive partner throughout Dan's football career, providing encouragement and stability as he navigated the demands of professional football and coaching.

Children: Dan and Holly Campbell have three children, who are an important part of their family life. The couple's children are actively involved in sports and other activities, reflecting the family's strong commitment to athleticism and teamwork. Dan often emphasizes the importance of family time and the role his children play in his life, balancing the demands of his coaching career with his responsibilities as a father.

Personal Interests and Hobbies

Outside of football, Dan Campbell has a variety of personal interests and hobbies that offer a glimpse into his personality and passions. His interests reflect a well-rounded individual with a love for the outdoors and a commitment to personal well-being.

Outdoor Activities: Campbell is an avid outdoorsman, enjoying activities such as hunting and fishing. His love for the outdoors is rooted in his upbringing in rural Texas and his appreciation for nature. These activities provide him with a sense of relaxation and enjoyment, offering a balance to the intensity of his coaching career.

Community Involvement: Dan Campbell is also known for his commitment to community service and philanthropy. He has been involved in various charitable initiatives, including supporting local youth programs and participating in fundraising events. His involvement in community activities reflects his belief in giving back and making a positive impact beyond the football field.

Personal Philosophy: Campbell's personal philosophy is deeply influenced by his upbringing and experiences in football. He values hard work, resilience, and integrity, and these principles guide both his professional and personal life. His approach to coaching and leadership is informed by his belief in the importance of character, discipline, and teamwork.

Dan Campbell's personal life and family background have had a significant impact on his career and approach to coaching. His strong family values, commitment to community service, and personal interests all contribute to his identity as a coach and leader. His experiences growing up in a small town, combined with his dedication to his family and personal passions, have shaped his approach to football and his role as a mentor and leader.

In summary, Dan Campbell's personal life and family background provide a rich context for understanding the man behind the coach. His close-knit family, personal interests, and commitment to community service reflect his values and character. As he continues his coaching career, Campbell's personal experiences and relationships remain integral to his approach to leadership and his impact on the sport.

CHAPTER FIVE: Philanthropy and Community Involvement

Dan Campbell's commitment to philanthropy and community involvement extends beyond his role as a football coach, reflecting his deep-seated values of service, integrity, and community spirit. His efforts to give back and make a positive impact have been a significant part of his life, influencing both his personal and professional endeavors.

Early Community Engagement

From an early age, Dan Campbell was influenced by the values of community support and service. Growing up in Clifton, Texas, he witnessed firsthand the importance of community bonds and mutual assistance. These early experiences shaped his belief in the importance of giving back and helping those in need. His upbringing instilled a sense of responsibility to contribute positively to society, a principle he has carried with him throughout his career.

Charitable Initiatives and Fundraising

Dan Campbell's philanthropic efforts have been diverse, ranging from supporting local youth programs to participating in high-profile fundraising events. His involvement in these initiatives underscores his commitment to making a tangible difference in the lives of others.

1. Supporting Youth Programs: Campbell has been actively involved in supporting youth programs and initiatives aimed at providing opportunities for young people. He has participated in events designed to promote youth sports, education, and personal development. His involvement often includes hosting football clinics, providing mentorship, and fundraising for local youth organizations. These efforts reflect his belief in the power of sports to inspire and shape young lives.

2. Charity Events and Fundraisers: Throughout his coaching career, Campbell has participated in various charity events and fundraisers. These events often focus on raising funds for causes such as cancer research, homelessness, and veterans' services. Campbell's participation in these events highlights his commitment to

supporting important causes and leveraging his platform to bring attention to critical issues.

3. Community Outreach: Campbell has also been involved in community outreach efforts, including partnerships with local organizations and charities. His work with these groups often involves direct interaction with community members, providing support, and contributing to initiatives that address pressing social issues. Campbell's engagement in community outreach reflects his belief in the importance of building strong, supportive communities.

Personal Projects and Contributions

In addition to his involvement in organized charitable efforts, Dan Campbell has undertaken personal projects that align with his values of service and community support. These projects often reflect his passion for making a positive impact in the lives of individuals and families.

1. Mentoring and Coaching: Campbell's role as a mentor extends beyond the football field. He has provided guidance and support to young athletes and aspiring coaches, sharing his knowledge and experiences to help them achieve their goals. His mentoring efforts often involve one-on-one interactions, offering valuable insights and encouragement to those pursuing careers in sports and beyond.

2. Community Service: Campbell's commitment to community service is evident in his participation in local service projects and events. He has been involved in activities such as organizing food drives, participating in

community clean-up efforts, and supporting local shelters. These activities demonstrate his dedication to addressing community needs and making a positive impact in everyday life.

Dan Campbell's philanthropic and community involvement reflects a broader commitment to service and positive impact. His efforts to support youth programs, participate in charitable events, and engage in community outreach contribute to his legacy as a coach and community leader. Campbell's dedication to giving back and making a difference underscores his belief in the importance of contributing to the greater good and using his platform for positive change.

The impact of Dan Campbell's philanthropic efforts is evident in the numerous individuals and communities he has touched. His involvement in supporting youth, contributing to charitable causes, and engaging in community service has made a significant difference in the lives of many. Campbell's approach to philanthropy is characterized by a genuine desire to help others and a commitment to addressing important social issues.

Dan Campbell's philanthropy and community involvement are integral to his identity as a coach and leader. His dedication to giving back, supporting important causes, and engaging with his community reflects his deep-seated values and commitment to making a positive impact. Through his various efforts, Campbell continues to inspire and contribute to the well-being of others, leaving a lasting legacy of service and community support.

CHAPTER SIX: Legacy and Impact

Dan Campbell's legacy and impact are defined by his journey from a tough, reliable NFL player to a dynamic and influential head coach. His contributions to the sport of football, his approach to leadership, and his commitment to community service collectively shape the enduring mark he has left on the game and those around him.

Football Legacy

1. Playing Career: Dan Campbell's playing career was characterized by his toughness, versatility, and leadership. Known for his exceptional blocking skills and resilience, Campbell earned respect as a reliable tight end

who could be counted on in crucial moments. His contributions were pivotal in key games, including his role in the New York Giants' Super Bowl XXXV run and his time with the Dallas Cowboys and Detroit Lions. His playing career set the foundation for his transition to coaching, highlighting his deep understanding of the game and his ability to perform under pressure.

2. Coaching Philosophy: As a coach, Campbell's philosophy is marked by an emphasis on physicality, discipline, and emotional intelligence. His approach to coaching integrates the lessons learned from his playing days and his experiences under influential mentors. Campbell's focus on building a strong team culture, fostering resilience, and promoting accountability has been a significant aspect of his coaching style. His ability to connect with

players on a personal level and inspire them to perform at their best has been central to his impact as a coach.

3. Influence on the Detroit Lions: Since becoming the head coach of the Detroit Lions, Campbell has worked to transform the team's culture and approach. His leadership has been instrumental in reshaping the team's identity, focusing on physical play, competitive spirit, and a positive mindset. His tenure has been marked by efforts to rebuild and reestablish the Lions as a competitive force in the NFL. Campbell's impact on the team is evident in the improved performance and renewed energy within the franchise.

Leadership and Personal Impact

1. Inspiring Leadership: Dan Campbell's leadership style is characterized by passion, authenticity, and a deep commitment to his players. His ability to inspire and motivate has earned him the respect and admiration of those around him. Campbell's leadership extends beyond the football field, influencing his players' personal development and professional growth. His emphasis on honesty, hard work, and team unity reflects his belief in the power of positive leadership and its impact on achieving success.

2. Mentoring and Development: Campbell's dedication to mentoring and developing young players and coaches has been a significant aspect of his career. His role as a mentor involves sharing his knowledge, providing guidance, and offering support to help others reach their full potential. His approach to coaching emphasizes

the importance of personal development, both on and off the field, contributing to the growth and success of those he works with.

Community Contributions

1. Philanthropy and Service: Dan Campbell's commitment to philanthropy and community service has been a defining aspect of his legacy. His involvement in supporting youth programs, participating in charitable events, and engaging in community outreach reflects his dedication to making a positive impact. Campbell's efforts to give back and contribute to the well-being of others demonstrate his belief in the importance of service and community support.

2. Positive Influence: Campbell's contributions to his community extend beyond organized

charitable efforts. His personal involvement in local projects, mentoring, and community service reflects a broader commitment to creating positive change. His impact is seen in the lives of individuals and communities he has supported, showcasing his dedication to making a meaningful difference.

Enduring Impact

Dan Campbell's legacy and impact are defined by his contributions to football, his leadership style, and his commitment to community service. His journey from player to coach, his innovative approach to leadership, and his dedication to supporting others collectively shape his enduring influence. Campbell's ability to inspire, motivate, and lead has left a lasting mark on the sport and the people he has worked with.

Dan Campbell's legacy is a testament to his dedication, passion, and impact. His contributions to football, his approach to leadership, and his commitment to community service reflect a career defined by excellence and positive influence. As he continues to lead and inspire, Campbell's legacy will be remembered for its impact on the game, its players, and the broader community.

Influence on Players and Coaching Staff

Dan Campbell's influence on players and coaching staff extends far beyond his role as a head coach. His approach to leadership, mentorship, and team dynamics has made a significant impact on those who work with him, shaping their development and contributing to their success both on and off the field.

Influence on Players
1. Leadership and Motivation: Dan Campbell's leadership style is marked by an intense passion for the game and a deep commitment to his players. His ability to inspire and motivate has been a key factor in his influence on players. Campbell's energetic and enthusiastic approach

creates an environment where players feel driven to give their best effort. His famous press conference, where he promised the team would "bite a kneecap off" if knocked down, epitomizes his motivational tactics and his ability to rally his players.

2. Personal Development: Campbell places a strong emphasis on personal development and growth. He takes a hands-on approach to mentoring, working closely with players to help them improve their skills and reach their full potential. His coaching philosophy includes a focus on developing both the physical and mental aspects of a player's game. By providing individualized attention and constructive feedback, Campbell helps players enhance their performance and build confidence.

3. Building Relationships: One of Campbell's strengths is his ability to build strong, personal relationships with players. He invests time in understanding their motivations, challenges, and aspirations. This personalized approach fosters trust and respect, creating a supportive environment where players feel valued and understood. Campbell's emphasis on open communication and genuine connections helps players feel more engaged and committed to the team's goals.

4. Resilience and Toughness: Campbell's own experiences as a player have shaped his approach to building resilience and toughness in his players. He encourages them to embrace challenges and persevere through difficult situations. His focus on mental toughness and a never-give-up attitude is designed to prepare

players for the rigors of professional football and to instill a strong work ethic.

Influence on Coaching Staff

1. Collaborative Environment: Dan Campbell fosters a collaborative and inclusive environment among his coaching staff. He values input from his assistants and encourages open dialogue and idea-sharing. This collaborative approach not only enhances the team's strategic planning but also helps develop the coaching staff's skills and knowledge. Campbell's willingness to listen and consider diverse perspectives contributes to a more dynamic and effective coaching staff.

2. Mentorship and Development: Campbell is committed to the professional development of his coaching staff. He serves as a mentor,

offering guidance and support to help them grow in their roles. His experience and insights provide valuable learning opportunities for his assistants, contributing to their development as coaches. Campbell's emphasis on continuous improvement and learning helps elevate the overall quality of the coaching staff.

3. Strategic Insights: As a coach with extensive playing experience, Campbell provides valuable strategic insights to his staff. His deep understanding of the game and its nuances informs his approach to game planning and strategy. By sharing his knowledge and perspectives, Campbell helps his coaching staff develop a more comprehensive understanding of football and improve their ability to make strategic decisions.

4. Building a Positive Culture: Campbell's leadership extends to creating a positive and supportive culture within the coaching staff. He emphasizes the importance of teamwork, mutual respect, and a shared commitment to the team's goals. This positive culture fosters a sense of unity and collaboration among the coaching staff, contributing to a more effective and harmonious working environment.

Impact on Team Dynamics

1. Enhancing Team Cohesion: Campbell's influence on both players and coaching staff contributes to overall team cohesion. His emphasis on building strong relationships, fostering open communication, and promoting a positive culture helps create a unified and motivated team. The sense of camaraderie and

shared purpose that Campbell cultivates is crucial for achieving success on the field.

2. Instilling a Winning Mentality: Campbell's approach to coaching instills a winning mentality within the team. His focus on resilience, toughness, and a never-give-up attitude influences both players and coaches, contributing to a competitive and determined mindset. This mentality is essential for overcoming challenges and striving for excellence in every aspect of the game.

Dan Campbell's influence on players and coaching staff is profound and multifaceted. His leadership, personal connections, and commitment to development shape the experiences and growth of those around him. By fostering a collaborative environment, providing mentorship, and emphasizing resilience, Campbell's impact extends beyond the football field, contributing to the overall success and cohesion of his team. His ability to inspire and motivate, combined with his strategic insights and positive culture, defines his lasting influence on the sport and the individuals he works with.

Media and Public Perception

Dan Campbell's media presence and public perception are as dynamic and multifaceted as his career itself. Known for his unorthodox approach and charismatic personality, Campbell has garnered significant attention both for his coaching style and his candidness. His media interactions and public image reflect his unique approach to leadership and his impact on the sport.

1. Charismatic Personality: Dan Campbell's media presence is marked by his larger-than-life personality and straightforward communication style. His ability to connect with the media through authentic and engaging interactions has made him a notable figure in sports journalism.

His energetic demeanor and willingness to speak candidly contribute to a memorable and often entertaining media presence.

2. Memorable Press Conferences: Campbell's press conferences are particularly notable for their candidness and unconventional approach. His memorable statements, such as the "bite a kneecap off" comment, have become defining moments in his media career. These statements, while sometimes controversial, highlight his passionate and unapologetic style, capturing the attention of both fans and the media.

3. Transparency and Honesty: One of Campbell's defining traits in media interactions is his transparency and honesty. He is known for addressing issues openly and providing straightforward answers to questions. This

approach has earned him respect for his authenticity and willingness to engage in meaningful discussions, even when the topics are challenging or uncomfortable.

4. Media Coverage and Narrative: Campbell's unconventional style and colorful personality have influenced the media narrative surrounding him. While some media coverage focuses on his bold and often unconventional statements, others highlight his dedication, work ethic, and commitment to building a successful team. This multifaceted media portrayal contributes to a nuanced public perception of Campbell.

Public Perception and Fan Reaction

1. Popularity and Fan Engagement: Dan Campbell's public perception is characterized by

a high level of popularity among fans. His enthusiastic and relatable approach to coaching resonates with many supporters, creating a strong connection with the fan base. Campbell's ability to engage with fans through his charismatic personality and relatable comments contributes to his widespread appeal.

2. Impact on Team Morale: Campbell's public image has a direct impact on team morale and fan support. His energetic and motivational style helps create a positive atmosphere both within the team and among supporters. Fans appreciate his commitment to the team and his ability to articulate a clear vision for success, which contributes to a sense of optimism and excitement.

3. Criticism and Challenges: Like many public figures, Campbell has faced criticism and challenges related to his media presence and coaching decisions. Critics may focus on aspects of his unconventional approach or specific decisions made during games. However, Campbell's ability to handle criticism with composure and his focus on continuous improvement help mitigate negative perceptions and maintain a positive public image.

4. Influence on Team Identity: Campbell's media presence and public perception have influenced the identity of the Detroit Lions. His passionate and bold approach contributes to the team's brand and narrative, shaping how the franchise is viewed by fans and the media. Campbell's emphasis on toughness, resilience, and

authenticity aligns with the team's efforts to redefine its identity and build a new reputation.

Media Strategies and Communication

1. Engaging with the Media: Campbell's media strategies involve direct and engaging communication. He often uses press conferences, interviews, and public appearances to share his thoughts, strategies, and vision for the team. His ability to articulate his ideas and connect with the media helps shape the narrative around the team and his coaching approach.

2. Leveraging Media for Positive Impact: Campbell uses media interactions to promote positive aspects of the team and its culture. By focusing on team achievements, player development, and community involvement, he

leverages media opportunities to highlight the positive impact of his coaching and the progress of the team.

3. Balancing Public and Private Life: Campbell's approach to managing his media presence involves balancing his public persona with his private life. While he is open and engaging in media interactions, he also maintains a level of privacy regarding personal matters. This balance helps preserve a clear distinction between his professional and personal life, allowing him to focus on his role as a coach while managing public expectations.

Dan Campbell's media presence and public perception reflect his distinctive coaching style and charismatic personality. His memorable press conferences, transparent communication, and engagement with fans contribute to a complex and multifaceted public image. While facing both praise and criticism, Campbell's ability to connect with the media and maintain a positive narrative helps shape his legacy and impact on the sport. His media interactions and public persona play a significant role in defining how he is perceived and the influence he has on fans, the team, and the broader football community.

Printed in Great Britain
by Amazon